W9-ABN-886

#23.00

AUG   2010

We Go!

Trucks

Dana Meachen Rau

Marshall Cavendish
Benchmark
New York

We go in a truck.

Trucks go in snow.

Trucks go in dirt.

Trucks go to fires.

Trucks carry garbage.

Trucks carry milk.

Trucks carry mail.

4306771

www.usps.com

www.usps.com

UNITED STATES
POSTAL SERVICE

Trucks carry hay.

We go in a truck!

Words to Know

dump truck

fire truck

garbage truck

hay truck

mail truck

milk truck

pickup truck

snow plow

Index

Page numbers in boldface are illustrations.

About the Author

Dana Meachen Rau is the author of many other titles in the Bookworms series, as well as other nonfiction and early reader books. She lives in Burlington, Connecticut, with her husband and two children.

With thanks to the Reading Consultants:

Nanci Vargus, Ed.D., is an Assistant Professor of Elementary Education at the University of Indianapolis.

Beth Walker Gambro is an Adjunct Professor at the University of Saint Francis in Joliet, Illinois.

23

Marshall Cavendish Benchmark
99 White Plains Road
Tarrytown, New York 10591-9001
www.marshallcavendish.us

Library of Congress Cataloging-in-Publication Data

Rau, Dana Meachen, 1971-
Trucks / by Dana Meachen Rau.
p. cm. — (Bookworms. We go!)
Includes index.
Summary: "Describes the physical attributes, different kinds, and purposes of trucks"—Provided by publisher.
ISBN 978-0-7614-4083-3
1. Trucks—Juvenile literature. I. Title.
TL230.15.R38 2010
629.224—dc22
2008042511

Editor: Christina Gardeski
Publisher: Michelle Bisson
Designer: Virginia Pope
Art Director: Anahid Hamparian

Photo Research by Anne Burns Images

Cover Photo by *Corbis*/Car Culture

The photographs in this book are used with permission and through the courtesy of:
Alamy Images: pp. 1, 15, 21TL Kim Karpeles; pp. 5, 21BR Simon Price; pp. 7, 20TL Greenshoots Communications;
pp. 9, 20TR Kevin Foy; pp. 11, 20BL Dennis MacDonald; pp. 13, 21TR Mark Boulton.
Photo Edit, Inc.: p. 3 Michelle Bridwell. *SuperStock*: pp. 17, 20BR age fotostock.
Corbis: pp. 19, 21BL Heide Benser/zefa.

Printed in Malaysia
1 3 5 6 4 2